## AVAILABLE:

SATB Director's Score (CMM02104)
SATB Singer's Edition (CMM02104S)
Three-Part Mixed Director's Score (CMM02105)
Three-Part Mixed Singer's Edition (CMM02105S)
Two-Part Director's Score (CMM02106)
Two-Part Singer's Edition (CMM02106S)
Instrumental Pak (CMM02104IN)
Listening CD (CMM02104CL)
Accompaniment CD (CMM02104CD)

Project Manager: TEENA CHINN
Production: MAUDLYN COOLEY
Cover Design: CANDY WOOLLEY

# GIVE OUR REGARDS TO BROADWAY

## Overture

SATB, accompanied

Original Words and Music by GEORGE M. COHAN
Additional Lyrics by TEENA CHINN
*Arranged by TEENA CHINN (ASCAP)*

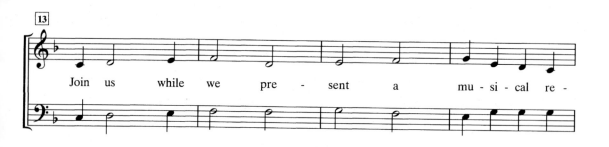

bur - lesque danc - - er. *Paint Your Wag-on* is a gold min-ing

spree._____ *My Fair La - dy,* E - li - za, is

coached by Hen - ry Hig - gins, P - H - D. A

*Fun - ny Thing Hap-pened At The Fo - rum* is a com - e - dy

set in an-cient Rome. Dor-'thy from Kan - sas

meets the Tin-man, and *The Wiz* of Oz helps her get home.

4

Hair tells a - bout the hip - pies, and in Wild - cat, they drill for liq - uid gold.

Fid - dler On The Roof is all a - bout tra - di - tion for young and old.

Zieg-field dis - cov - ered Fan - ny, the Fun - ny Girl, Miss Brice.

An - y - thing Goes is so much fun that it ap - peared on Broad - way

CMM02104S

twice. *Brig-a-doon* is a cit - y that ev-'ry hun-dred years comes a - live._____ Bob - by Child, in *Cra - zy For You,* puts on a show to help the play - house thrive. *Cam-e-lot* is the leg - end of King Ar - thur, *The Once and Fu - ture King.*_____ In *Bye Bye Bird - ie,* clean - cut kids love to hear Con-rad Bird - ie

set at Cat - fish Row. Hope-ful - ly ev - er - af - ter is *Sweet Char - i - ty*'s ba - sic theme in life._____ *Scar - let Pim - per - nel*'s main char - ac - ters are Percy and his wife. *E - vit - a*'s the true - life sto - ry of Ar - gen - tin - a's Ev - a Per - on._____ *An - nie*, the or - phan,

meets Dad-dy War-bucks and won't have to be a - lone._____

_____ Mam - ma Mi - a is three love sto - ries, set to

AB - BA hits in - clud-ing "Danc-ing Queen."

In - to The Woods has fair - y-tale char - ac-ters like

Snow White in each scene. Je - sus Christ

Su - per-star's an op - 'ra, with the mu - sic be - ing

# Medley I

SATB, accompanied

*Arranged by* TEENA CHINN

**"MY FAIR LADY"**
*I COULD HAVE DANCED ALL NIGHT*
Lyrics by ALAN JAY LERNER
Music by FREDERICK LOEWE

CMM02104S

**THE RAIN IN SPAIN**
Lyrics by ALAN JAY LERNER
Music by FREDERICK LOEWE
**Slow, in two (♩ = 56)**

Rain In Spain stays main - ly in the plain!_ The

*(end solo)* *(unis.)*

*(unis.)*
I think she's got it!

Rain in Spain stays main - ly in the plain! I have

*rit.*

**ON THE STREET WHERE YOU LIVE**
Lyrics by ALAN JAY LERNER
Music by FREDERICK LOEWE
**Moderately slow (♩ = 80)**

of - ten walked_____ down this street be - fore_____ But the

**54**
pave-ment al - ways stayed be - neath my feet be - fore._____ All at

**58**
once am I_____ sev -'ral sto - ries high._____ Know - ing

**62**
*rit.* (♩ = ♩)
I'm On The Street Where You Live. I've Grown Ac -
SOLO (opt. unis.) *mp*

**I'VE GROWN ACCUSTOMED TO HER FACE**
Lyrics by ALAN JAY LERNER
Music by FREDERICK LOEWE
**66** Slowly (♩ = 72)
cus - tomed To Her Face She al-most makes the day be - gin. *(end solo)*

(unis.) *mf* **70**
I was se - rene - ly in - de - pen-dent and con - tent be-fore we met;

Sure - ly I could al - ways be that way a - gain and yet, I've grown ac -

**GET ME TO THE CHURCH ON TIME**
Lyrics by ALAN JAY LERNER
Music by FREDERICK LOEWE

**Moderately fast (♩ = 120)**

cus-tomed to her looks; Ac-cus-tomed to her voice; Ac-cus-tomed to her face._____

I'm get-ting mar-ried in the morn-ing_____ Ding! dong! the bells are gon-na chime._____

Pull out the stop-per; Let's have a whop-per; But Get Me To The Church On Time!

**"A FUNNY THING HAPPENED ON THE WAY TO THE FORUM"**
*COMEDY TONIGHT*
Music and Lyrics by STEPHEN SONDHEIM

Some-thing fa-mil-iar, some-thing pe-cu-liar, Some-thing for

14

ev - 'ry-one, a com-e-dy to-night! Old sit - u - a - tions, new com - pli-ca-tions, Noth-ing por-ten-tous or po-lite;___ Trag-e-dy to-mor-row, com-e-dy to-night! Come on and

**"THE WIZ"**
*EASE ON DOWN THE ROAD*
Music and Lyrics by CHARLIE SMALLS
**Moderately (♩ = 90)**

ease on___ down, ease on down___ the road.___

Come on, ease on___ down, ease on down___ the road.___

Don't you car-ry noth-in' that might be a load.___ Come on,

**"PAINT YOUR WAGON"**
*THEY CALL THE WIND MARIA*
Lyrics by ALAN JAY LERNER
Music by FREDERICK LOEWE

*WAND'RIN' STAR*
Lyrics by ALAN JAY LERNER
Music by FREDERICK LOEWE

**143** I was born under a Wan - d'rin' Star.

**147** When I get to heav - en tie me to a tree, Or I'll be - gin to roam, And soon you know where I will be.

**151** I was born under a Wan - d'rin' Star, A

**155** *molto rit.* Wan - d'rin', Wan - d'rin' Star. Things look

**"GYPSY"**
*EVERYTHING'S COMING UP ROSES*
Lyrics by STEPHEN SONDHEIM
Music by JULE STYNE

**159** **Brightly (♩ = 128)** *f*

swell. Things look great. Gon - na

# Medley II
## SATB, accompanied

*Arranged by TEENA CHINN*

**Moderately, with a lilt (♩ = 126)**

**"FIDDLER ON THE ROOF"**
*IF I WERE A RICH MAN*
Lyrics by SHELDON HARNICK
Music by JERRY BOCK

**MATCHMAKER**
Lyrics by SHELDON HARNICK
Music by JERRY BOCK

© 1964 (Renewed 1992) MAYERLING PRODUCTIONS LTD. and JERRY BOCK ENTERPRISES

**SUNRISE, SUNSET**
Lyrics by SHELDON HARNICK
Music by JERRY BOCK

Sun - rise,_____ Sun - set. Sun - rise,_____ Sun - set.

*cresc.*
Swift - ly_____ fly the years;_____

*mf*
One sea - son fol - low-ing an - oth - er,

*rit.*
La - den with hap - pi - ness and tears.

**"FUNNY GIRL"**
*PEOPLE*
Words by BOB MERRILL
Music by JULE STYNE

Slowly ( ♩ = 76)
SOLO (or opt. unis.)
Peo - ple,_____ peo - ple who need peo - ple_____ Are the

luck - i - est peo - ple_____ in the world._____ We're

**69**

chil - dren_____ need - ing oth - er chil - dren_____ And yet,

**73**

let - ting our grown - up pride Hide all the need in - side. Act - ing

**77**

more like chil - dren, than chil - dren.

(♩ = ♪)

***DON'T RAIN ON MY PARADE***
Words by BOB MERRILL
Music by JULE STYNE
**Moderately fast (♩ = 76)**

**81**

(unis.) *mf*

Don't tell_ me not to_ fly. I've sim - ply got to.
Don't tell_ me not to_ live, just sit and put - ter.

**85**

If some - one takes a_ spill, it's me and not you. Don't bring_ a - round a_
Life's can - dy and the_ sun's a ball of but - ter. Who told_ you you're al -

< *f*

— cloud To rain on my pa - rade._____
- lowed to rain on my pa -

"HAIR"
*AQUARIUS*

Moderately fast (♩ = 144)

Music by GALT MACDERMOT
Words by JAMES RADO and GEROME RAGNI

**LET THE SUNSHINE IN**
Music by GALT MACDERMOT
Words by JAMES RADO and GEROME RAGNI

**"ANYTHING GOES"**
*ANYTHING GOES*
Words and Music by COLE PORTER

24

BLOW, GABRIEL, BLOW
Words and Music by COLE PORTER

HEY, LOOK ME OVER
Music by CY COLEMAN
Lyrics by CAROLYN LEIGH

# Medley III
## SATB, accompanied

*Arranged by TEENA CHINN*

"BYE BYE BIRDIE"
*PUT ON A HAPPY FACE*
Music by CHARLES STROUSE
Lyric by LEE ADAMS

CMM02104S

**"CAMELOT"**
*CAMELOT*
Lyrics by ALAN KAY LERNER
Music by FREDERICK LOEWE

**"FINIAN'S RAINBOW"**
*LOOK TO THE RAINBOW*
Words by E.Y. HARBURG
Music by BURTON LANE

"CRAZY FOR YOU"
*I GOT RHYTHM*
Music and Lyrics by
GEORGE GERSHWIN and IRA GERSHWIN

© 1930 WB MUSIC CORP. (Renewed)

**SOMEONE TO WATCH OVER ME**
Music and Lyrics by
GEORGE GERSHWIN and IRA GERSHWIN

Lyrics: find him__ 'Round__ my door. I__ got star-light,__ I__ got sweet dreams,__ I__ got my man__ Who could ask for an-y-thing more, Who could ask for an-y-thing more?

There's a some-bod-y I'm long-ing to see. I hope that he Turns out to be Some-one who'll watch o-ver me.

### THEY CAN'T TAKE THAT AWAY FROM ME
Music and Lyrics by
GEORGE GERSHWIN and IRA GERSHWIN

### EMBRACEABLE YOU
Music and Lyrics by
GEORGE GERSHWIN and IRA GERSHWIN

**144**

Em-brace me, You ir-re-

**148** *mf*

place - a - ble you! Don't be a

naugh - ty ba - by, Come to pa-pa, Come to pa-pa, do!

**152** *mp* rit. *mf* (♩ = ♩)

My sweet em-brace-a-ble you! What a

**"BRIGADOON"**
*ALMOST LIKE BEING IN LOVE*
Lyrics by ALAN JAY LERNER
Music By FREDERICK LOEWE

**156** Moderately (♩ = 80)  **160**

day this has been! What a rare mood I'm in! Why, it's al-most like

**164**

be - ing in love. There's a smile on my face for the

**168**

whole hu-man race. Why, it's al-most like be-ing in love!

**"42ND STREET"**
*FORTY-SECOND STREET*
Music by HARRY WARREN
Words by AL DUBIN

**172** Moderately fast (♩ = 92)

Come and meet____ those danc-ing feet,____ on the

**176**

av-e-nue I'm tak-ing you to,____ For-ty Sec-ond Street.

**180**

Hear the beat____ of danc-ing feet,____ it's the

Hear the beat____ of danc-ing feet,

**184**

song I love the mel-o-dy of,___ For-ty Second Street.

*LULLABY OF BROADWAY*
Music by HARRY WARREN
Words by AL DUBIN

**188** (♩ = 84)

*f*

Come on a-long and lis-ten to___ the lul-la-by of Broad-way.

*f*

# Medley IV
## SATB, accompanied

*Arranged by TEENA CHINN*

**"BARNUM"**
***COME FOLLOW THE BAND***
Music by CY COLEMAN
Lyrics by MICHAEL STEWART

This Arrangement © 2002 by NOTABLE MUSIC CO., INC., WB MUSIC CORP., KNIGHT ERRANT MUSIC,
SCARAMANGA MUSIC, BRONX FLASH MUSIC, INC., EVITA MUSIC LTD./UNIVERSAL - MCA MUSIC PUBLISHING,
GEORGE GERSHWIN MUSIC, IRA GERSHWIN MUSIC,
DuBOSE and DOROTHY HEYWARD MEMORIAL FUND and LIDA ENTERPRISES, INC.
All Rights Reserved including Public Performance

36

**THERE IS A SUCKER BORN EV'RY MINUTE**
Music by CY COLEMAN
Lyrics by MICHAEL STEWART

**THE COLORS OF MY LIFE**
Music by CY COLEMAN
Lyrics by MICHAEL STEWART

catch the light. Is there a sight that's sweet-er than that?

There is a suck-er born ev-'ry min-ute, And friends the big-gest one ex-clud-in' none is me! The Col-ors Of My Life are boun-ti-ful and bold, The pur-ple glow of in-di-go the gleam of green and gold.

CMM02104S

© 1980 NOTABLE MUSIC CO., INC.
All Rights Administered by WB MUSIC CORP.

SOLO *(opt. unis.)*
*molto rit.* **mp**

thanks for the glo - ri - ous fight!  When I

### WHEN I LOOK AT YOU
Lyrics by NAN KNIGHTON
Music by FRANK WILDHORN
**64** **Slow, with feeling ( ♩ = 68)**

look at you,  he is touch - ing me.  I would reach for him, but who can hold a

*(end solo)* *(unis.)* **68**

mem - o - ry?  And love is - n't ev - 'ry - thing,  That

*(unis.)* **mp**

*accel.*

moon - light on the bed will melt a - way,  some_ day.  Where's the girl?_
**mf** SOLO *(opt. unis.)*

### WHERE'S THE GIRL?
Lyrics by NAN KNIGHTON
**72** Music by FRANK WILDHORN
**Moderately fast ( ♩ = 108)**

Is she gaz - ing at me_ with sur - prise?_  Do I still_

**77**

_ see that blaze_ in her eyes?  Am I dream - ing, or is_ she be - side  me

*I GOT PLENTY O' NUTTIN'*
By GEORGE GERSHWIN, DuBOSE and DOROTHY HEYWARD
and IRA GERSHWIN

"SWEET CHARITY"
*I'M A BRASS BAND*
Music by CY COLEMAN
Lyrics by DOROTHY FIELDS

*BIG SPENDER*
Music by CY COLEMAN
Lyrics by DOROTHY FIELDS

42

woul-dn't you like to know what's go-ing on in my mind? So let me get

**152**

right to the point, I don't pop my cork for ev-'ry guy I see.

**156** *(Sop. div.)*

Hey! Big Spend-er, spend

*IF MY FRIENDS COULD SEE ME NOW!*

**162** Music by CY COLEMAN
Lyrics by DOROTHY FIELDS

Brightly (♩ = 106)

a lit-tle time with me. If they could see me now,

**166**

my lit-tle dust-y group, Traip-sin' 'round this mil-lion dol-lar

**170**

chick-en coop. I'd like those stum-ble bums to see for a fact

CMM02104S

# Medley V
## SATB, accompanied

*Arranged by TEENA CHINN*

**"ANNIE"**
*YOU'RE NEVER FULLY DRESSED WITHOUT A SMILE*
Music by CHARLES STROUSE
Lyric by MARTIN CHARNIN

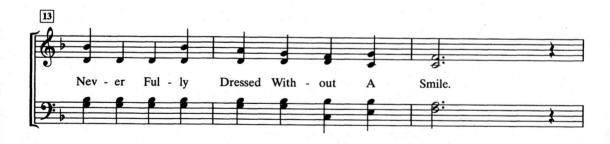

*TOMORROW*
Music by CHARLES STROUSE
Lyric by MARTIN CHARNIN

*IT'S THE HARD-KNOCK LIFE*
Music by CHARLES STROUSE
Lyric by MARTIN CHARNIN

CMM02104S

46

**MAYBE**
Music by CHARLES STROUSE
Lyric by MARTIN CHARNIN

**"INTO THE WOODS"**
*CHILDREN WILL LISTEN*
Music and Lyrics by STEPHEN SONDHEIM

"JESUS CHRIST SUPERSTAR"
*I DON'T KNOW HOW TO LOVE HIM*
Music by ANDREW LLOYD WEBBER
Words by TIM RICE

**"MAMMA MIA"**
*MAMMA MIA*
Words and Music by BENNY ANDERSSON,
STIG ANDERSON and BJORN ULVAEUS

**DANCING QUEEN**
Words and Music by BENNY ANDERSSON,
STIG ANDERSON and BJORN ULVAEUS

**"RAGTIME"**
*WHEELS OF A DREAM*
Words by LYNN AHRENS
Music by STEPHEN FLAHERTY

50

RAGTIME
Words by LYNN AHRENS
Music by STEPHEN FLAHERTY

CMM02104S

**MAKE THEM HEAR YOU**
Words by LYNN AHRENS
Music by STEPHEN FLAHERTY

la! And there was dis - tant mu - sic, sim - ple and some - how sub - lime, giv - ing the na - tion a new syn - co - pa - tion. The peo - ple called it Rag - time!

**Slowly with emotion (♩ = 80)**

Go out and tell our sto - ry. Let it ech - o far and wide. Make them hear you. Make them hear you. How jus - tice was our bat - tle and how jus - tice was de - nied. Make them hear you. Make them hear you. And